AN AFRICAN ROCK
Copyright © 2020 by Doris Dean Hannah Turner
ISBN 978-1-7345235-0-8 (Paperback)
ISBN 978-1-7345235-1-5 (Hardcover)

Designed and Published by King's Daughter Publishing
Indian Trail, North Carolina 28079
www.KingsDaughterPublishing.com

All rights reserved. No part of this publication may be reproduced, stored in a retrieval system or transmitted, in any form or by any means, electronic, mechanical, photocopying, recording or otherwise, without permission in writing from the author.

Printed in the United States of America.

TABLE OF CONTENTS

Dedication	5
Acknowledgements	7

UPENDO (LOVE)

Love in a Time Capsule	10
Timeless Rhyme	11
Brighter Days Ahead	12
Wait	13
How to Escape an Aching Heart	15
Imprint on My Heart	16

HUZUNI (LOSS)

Before I Close My Eyes	18
His Diamond	20
Don't Shed Any Tears	21
Embedded in My Heart	22
Don't Look at Me Now	23

URITHY (LEGACY)

Stories of Old	26
If I Knew What I Know Now	27
Through Daddy's Eyes	29
Grandmother	30
Summer of 1973	32
Uncle James	34
My South African Family (The Oliver's)	36
Mama Didn't Take No Stuff	38
Sometimes When I Look in the Mirror	40
Mothers	42

TABLE OF CONTENTS

MAISHA (LIFE)

I Was Born Three Times	44
Reaching and Grabbing at Me	45
An African Rock	46
Memories That Cannot Be Erased	48
Time Doesn't Wait on No One	49
A Taste of South Africa	51
A South African Tree	53
The Nature of Life	54
The Ocean	55
Never Turn Your Back on the Ocean	56
Swish, Swish, Swish	57
Lord, I am Not Perfect	58
The Chains of Life	59
Resilient	60
Thanksgiving	61
Courage to Be Free	63
A Rose	65
Our Pastor is Human	66
Who	67
About the Author	68

DEDICATION

This book of poetry is a collection of poems spanning over 40 years. It has been an awesome journey of my life to convey some of my experiences, thoughts and the meaning of just living life.

It is my distinguished honor to dedicate this collection of poetry to the memory of my late husband, Michael Leon Turner, Sr. He allowed me to grow and explore life and never stopped me from pursuing my dreams. He was my friend and love for 44 years until he was called from his earthly home to his heavenly home in 2019.

ACKNOWLEDGEMENTS

I want to extend special thanks to my children, Michael Jr., Samuel and Phyllis. I am so proud of you and love you with all of my heart.

My brother Johnny, you mean more to me than you will ever know. My Kenyan brother Ransome, thank you for your friendship and support through the years.

My nieces, Alesada and Zharia, you have made an imprint of love I can't find words to express.

My cousin Marlon, for your unique gifts and talents you share with me. Pearl, my South African daughter, for inviting me to visit her home and family in Cape Town, South Africa.

I want to extend my sincere appreciation to all my family and friends who have spoken words of encouragement in each of my many endeavors. I love you more than you know!

Finally, Anderson, thank you for being a part of my next chapter, "Brighter Days Ahead."

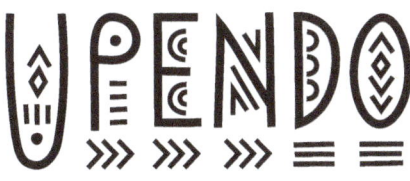

"LOVE"

 AN AFRICAN ROCK

LOVE IN A TIME CAPSULE

Love in a time capsule…
We put our hearts into it.

To capture some of the memories
We shall never forget.

Poems, letters, pictures
and memorabilia inside.

Sealed with Hershey's Kisses of love
Wrapped in silver foil.

Love in a time capsule…
Thrown into the Atlantic Sea;
All the way in Africa
The land of our people, you see.

Don't be afraid
To release your love in a time capsule.

Because, sure enough
One day, love in a time capsule you will see.

Someone will find it
When it comes back from the Atlantic Sea.

TIMELESS RHYME

My emotions are a timeless rhyme
That causes tears to flow down my cheeks.

To have a friend in whom I can confide;
To share my most intimate thoughts;
Makes me feel the warmth from within.

A touch, a kiss, a warm embrace
Sending emotions as if they're running a race.

Just to rub your face
Is comforting in every way.

The look of love I see in your eyes
Follows me when we're apart.

You have captured my heart
With your patience and listening ear;
Draws me forever near.

A friendship is one of the greatest loves
That can ever be shared;
While the purity at which it's given beats
A timeless rhyme.

 AN AFRICAN ROCK

BRIGHTER DAYS AHEAD

Candy apples, hayrides in Ypsilanti,
Was my first time getting a call from you.

Teary-eyed walking through the space of land
Wondering when would my eyes dry.

Joy, laughter and sharing my memories of him with you
Eases the pain and helps me walk through
The Journey of Life that seemed so empty.
Words of wisdom that helps me float through.

Sunshine and brighter days have broken through.
Thank you, God, for ordering my path in this direction
To help me along the way.

Though my heart shall never forget the love that I shared,
It helped me put my life in perspective
As I travel, dear Lord, this journey of life with you.

WAIT

I love you with the passion
Of a flaming fire.

I love you like the never ending water
That flows from Niagara Falls.

I love you like a roaring lion,
Calling for his mate.

I love you like a runner sprinting for the finish line—
Sweating, and stretching with every
Beam of his body.

I love you like a football player
Ready to tackle his opponent.

I love you like butter melting
In a skillet.

Like gravy being poured
On top of mashed potatoes
And then being sopped up with a biscuit.

Longing to be near you
With every beat of my heart.
With a thirst that will never stop.

With every quench of my being,
Waiting to consummate.

AN AFRICAN ROCK

When we shall become one
And the passion of that flaming fire
Will be worth the wait and shall never go out.

HOW TO ESCAPE AN ACHING HEART

How do you escape an aching heart?

Do you fly across the sky or take a trip out to sea?

Do you search for something to replace it?
Maybe shopping or maybe food?

You can only escape an aching heart
For just a moment or two until it starts to creep
Back upon you.

How do you escape an aching heart?

Look at it in the eye.

Face it. Deal with it.

And one day you will be able to face the pain
Of an aching heart
That built up inside of you.

Until one day you will realize it's time
To let it go.

IMPRINT ON MY HEART

You made an imprint on my heart
The day I met you
That's tattooed with love.

Your embrace and tender touch
Will forever leave marks
That can never be erased.

Some days, my heart aches when I think of you.
Not from sadness, but from pure joy
From sharing a life with you.

Love of a lifetime, is something some people
never experience.
But you and I had a lifetime of love that was
Sanctioned by the Holy Spirit.
This experience certainly made an imprint on
My heart.

Faithfulness, honesty, trust, security and fulfillment.
All which is built on a foundation
Of our love for Christ.

You made an imprint on my heart.

HUZINI

"LOSS"

 AN AFRICAN ROCK

BEFORE I CLOSE MY EYES

Before I close my eyes…

Tell me that you love me
Before I close my eyes.

Let me feel your warm embrace
While blood is still flowing through my veins.

Let me smell the flowers of life
While I can still inhale.

Let me hear your voice of laughter
While I can still hear.

Love is an action word that deserves
More than being with just a bunch of words.
So, let's show "love in action"
Like it's well-deserved.

Don't make a fuss to make me famous,
After I close my eyes.

Do it while I can still hear and be heard
Before I close my eyes.

Your touch, your smell, your actions of love;
Let me experience them please.

This is when it should be done.

Before I close my eyes.

Don't try to find closure and comfort
After I close my eyes.

Sit your ass down!
Nobody wants to hear your words.
It's too late!

I've done closed my eyes.

 AN AFRICAN ROCK

HIS DIAMOND

He knew she was his Diamond,
That surrounded his presence for many years.

She shined like the sun above the sky.

She was smooth and soft to the touch.

She was the most precious love of his life.

He wanted to be in her presence all the time,
But sometimes life happens beyond our control.

There she was, his most precious love of a lifetime.
She was left to move on alone.

She was left for another.

His most precious love.

His Diamond that he had to leave behind.

DON'T SHED ANY TEARS

Don't shed any tears for me,
No not one!

A smile, a visit, or "How are you today?"
Do you even care?

Don't shed any tears for me,
No not one!
I'm old and weary of this life.

I've lived, worked and I've done so many things
I regret.

Don't shed any tears for me,
No not one!

No money, no joy, no peace within.
Lord Jesus, will I ever have hope again?

I used to enjoy the simple things in life—a candy bar,
Watching TV or a walk to the corner store.

Don't shed any tears for me,
No not one!

Lord, take me.
There is nothing left for me on this Earth.

Don't shed any tears for me.
No. Not. One!

 AN AFRICAN ROCK

EMBEDDED IN MY HEART

Is he just a memory who is embedded in my heart?
So many years of love and embrace seems
As it has been torn from my heart.

Death is a part of life that we must accept.
But it doesn't erase the memories that are
Embedded in my heart.

Seeking and searching the next chapter of my life.
I must keep on moving, because he's still within my heart.

Embrace, accept, appreciate
The memories because they are precious and so alive.

Was he just a memory embedded in my heart?
I say, *"It's not just a memory because he is embedded
And tattooed across my heart."*

DON'T LOOK AT ME NOW

Don't look at me now that I am sleeping.
Oh, you said you saw me just a few years ago.

Don't look at me now.
Oh, you said you called me but you can't
Remember when.

You liked my page on Facebook.
You saw me on Instagram.
You messaged me a time or two.
Don't you know it's not the same?

Put those electronics down, and take some time today
To spend with your loved ones who helped you
Along the way.

You said that I am part of your family, but
When was the last time you reached out
And touched?

I was with you while you were growing up every
Step of the way.

Don't look at me now that I am sleeping.
You had your chance.
There is nothing that you can do or say.

URITHI

"LEGACY"

 AN AFRICAN ROCK

STORIES OF OLD

Don't let the stories of old
Die on you.

The stories of our ancestors
And of their youth.

Ask questions.
Don't be afraid.

Sit down.
Spend a little time.

Before you know it,
Time will pass you by
And those old stories
Will never be told.

DORIS DEAN HANNAH TURNER

IF I KNEW WHAT I KNOW NOW

If I knew what I know now,
I would have asked my grandmother
About how it was growing up in the South.

If I knew what I know now,
I would have sat at my grandmother's feet
Just to hear her hum the songs of old.

If I knew what I know now,
I would have been more attentive
To my surroundings and my family.
I would have seen them more often.

Now, I know what I know now.
I ask God daily to help me care
More about my ancestry
And the generations to come after me.

It seems as if each generation
Doesn't care about their ancestry.

I cried out,
"God please have mercy!
Help them to see.
If they don't begin to care,
What I know will be lost for eternity."

Now, I know what I know.

AN AFRICAN ROCK

I am responsible
For the knowledge
That is before me.

I have generations
And generations
That will come after me.

I am responsible to set history free.
Yes, I am responsible
To set history free.

Yes, *you* are responsible
To tell your children,
Your children's children,
Your nieces, your nephews
And all your family.

You, yes YOU, were chosen
To keep alive your family's history.

Ask the questions
You need answers to,
So that you will know now
What you need to know
About your history.

THROUGH DADDY'S EYES

No heart monitor.
No ventilator.
No nurses poking me.

Hallelujah!
Praise God, I'm free!

No Vicodin.
No Morphine.
And thank God,
No more suctioning.

Hallelujah!
Praise God, I'm free!

Jesus died on the cross
And rose just to set my soul free.

Hallelujah! Hallelujah!
Praise God, I'm Free!

 AN AFRICAN ROCK

GRANDMOTHER

Grandmother.

Quiet, sweet and humble too.
Rarely a mumbling word of complaint.

When we'd go to Grandmother's,
We would always race for leftover biscuits,
Bacon and sausage on the stove.

She even watched her grands—
And great-grandkids too—
Until she couldn't anymore.

Yes! She was understanding,
Generous, a peacemaker and faithful to her Lord.

Out of four generations left to follow her,
Not even one possessed
The special qualities of Grandmother.

Three scores and ten
Our Lord has promised his own.
But Grandmother, Grandmother
He gave you almost 20 more.

Her footsteps only got a little shorter
Just a few years ago.
But still down to Michelle's,
Her hairdresser, she would go.

DORIS DEAN HANNAH TURNER

Now, her daughter, Annie,
Would take her fishing,
Dining, garage sales and traveling South
With Mrs. Taylor, too.

Until the Lord said, *"Carrie Bell,
Slow down it's almost time to go."*

So she stayed awake for as long as she could,
Because Grandmother was very nosey.
We really couldn't keep anything from her.

God said, *"Carrie Bell, Carrie Bell,
Come on, it's time to go."*

So she shut her eyes Monday evening
With her heart open wide
And ready to be received.

"Oh, Lord!" she said.

*"Thank you for the life you have given me on
This Earth
To see my grands, greats and great-great
Grands too.
But hey y'all, I'd rather be with Jesus,
My Savior. Make sure you're living right
So that you can too."*

 AN AFRICAN ROCK

SUMMER OF 1973

10918 South Peoria, Chicago, Illinois
    Was the place for me in 1973.

Mom and I wasn't
    Communicating very well, you see.

As a teenager, it was very difficult for me,
    But Auntie knew just how to handle me.

She took the time to listen.
    She treated me like her daughter, the
    summer of 1973.

Reading and sewing were her hobbies.
    Cooking rice everyday was her specialty.

She taught me how to take the bus,
    Up and down Halsted Street every weekend
    To my cousins, who lived on Sangamon Street.

She had a heart of gold. It was called the gift of Ministry.
    Back and forth, wherever she could be of
    help, to her family.

Making sure her niece graduated was surly a Task, you see.

Auntie had a very friendly personality.
    A servant of God.
    Caring for his people was her calling,
most definitely.

It was wonderful spending time with Auntie
    The summer of 1973.

 AN AFRICAN ROCK

UNCLE JAMES

He was the last child born to Janie and Jerry.
He was raised by his brother, Freeman, and his
Wife, Ruby.

James earned his living by the sweat of his brow.
He was a strong, loving, caring, God-fearing
Black man.

I came to Mississippi in 1977.

That's when I remember meeting Uncle James
And Aunt Birdie,
With my husband by my side and a baby in
My arms.

Every time I came to Mississippi,
Up the hill I would run to see my Uncle James
And Aunt Birdie.

Oh! How excited I would be
To see them again.

When I called out his name,
I would fall in his arms.
He would give me a hug
With his big strong arms,
And a great big smile on his face—
Just grinning from ear-to-ear.

Now, Aunt Birdie's breakfast was the best I ever had.
Pear preserves, biscuits, grits, ham and eggs.
He was my Uncle James.
She was my Aunt Birdie.

Now, don't get mad.

I know they're your Uncle and Aunt too...
But I'm just making this personal just as
You would too.

 AN AFRICAN ROCK

MY SOUTH AFRICAN FAMILY (THE OLIVER'S)

Dottie loves her family. She has a heart of gold.
She's always in the kitchen
Whipping up a South African meal.
She's one of the best cooks in South Africa.

Tonya—she's smooth and easy going—right by
Her side.

Daryl, minding the oven, cooking crayfish
All the time.
He plays rugby. He's swift and fast, I can tell.

Pearl is busy catching up on her rest.
She's a truck driver like her father, which is
In her DNA.
I can see that very well.

Gram is busy smoking his cigarettes
And drinking coffee after every meal.
He works hard making a living
So his family can have the comforts of life.
He builds, fixes cars, and makes something
Out of nothing.
He has a vision that's out of this world.

Amy is very shy
And loves to watch television.
She's smart as a whip and manages school very well.

DORIS DEAN HANNAH TURNER

Caylum is very smart and busy, you see.
He's very helpful—Gram's first grandchild.
It makes him very happy
To have a male child to carry on his legacy
In this strange world.

Well! It's almost time to go back to America.

This is my South African family from across the sea.
They are very special to me.
We will meet again one day and share
The most precious memories of
Our times from across the sea.

 AN AFRICAN ROCK

MAMA DIDN'T TAKE NO STUFF

Daddy rarely disciplined us.

So, when we got out of hand,
Mama didn't take no stuff!

When we were children
She sung and read to us and
Then sent us to bed.

On Sunday morning,
She sent us through the fields on
Cole Chester Street, to catch the church bus

'Cause Mama didn't take no stuff!

She took us to pick beans on Sally and George's farm,
And taught us how to manage our time and funds

'Cause Mama didn't take no stuff!

"Wash clothes! Hang them on the clothes line!
Cook, wash dishes, and clean this house too!"

'Cause Mama didn't take no stuff!

She would cut her eyes at you,
And you knew what that meant.

DORIS DEAN HANNAH TURNER

She would raise her hands.
You better run as fast as you can!

'Cause Mama didn't take no stuff!

If you were bad in school
Or broke her rules?

Sure enough,
You would be across the street on
Oakley picking out your own switch

'Cause Mama didn't take no stuff!

So children, grand children and great-grands too
Please! Keep Mama's spirit alive in you.

'Cause Mama didn't take no stuff!

AN AFRICAN ROCK

SOMETIMES WHEN I LOOK IN THE MIRROR

Sometimes when I look in the mirror,
    I see my mother looking back at me.
    Would she be pleased with
    Who I have become in society?

Sometimes when I look in the mirror,
    I see my mother's thin hair,
    Her forehead and her features in me.

Sometimes when I look in the mirror,
    I see my mother's strength
    That she put inside of me.

The traveling she did extensively.
    Her strong desires.
    Who am I and where did I come from?
    And where, oh where, is all my parents'
    family?

Sometimes when I look in the mirror,
    I feel like an only child.
    No sisters to confide in.
    No sisters to enjoy each other's company.

Sometimes when I look in the mirror
    I understand that I am who I am
    And my mother's life is a part of me.
    The desire to do all that is within me.

DORIS DEAN HANNAH TURNER

She was loved by many
    Because of her personality.
    She reached out to all her friends and
    Family.

When I look in the mirror,
    I believe I see my mother staring back at me.
    Saying, *"Well-done, my daughter.*
    You are a lot like me."

MOTHERS

Mothers are the most beautiful creatures.
God made them with a thousand features.

Taxi cab drivers, nurses, teachers,
Chefs and tailors and even preachers.

Yes, mothers are the backbone to society.
When things go wrong, she is strong.

She encourages you when you're sad.
She helps to make you glad.

She prays for you
When you're sleeping.

When you just don't know
What to do,
She'll be your friend through and through.

A mother has
A lot of eyes.
Now her mind
Is on a thousand things at one time.

I wonder, I wonder, how she does it?

Only God knew what he was doing
When he made mothers.

MAISHA

"LIFE"

 AN AFRICAN ROCK

I WAS BORN THREE TIMES

The way I see it, I was born three times.

The first time
Is when I was pulled from my mother's womb
And the doctor slapped me on my behind.

The second time I was born,
Is when God saved my soul from eternal hell.
That was a wonderful experience
Because he cleansed my soul from within.

The third time I was born again was in 1988,
When I took a trip to Mississippi,
Where my father was pulled from his mother's womb
And was slapped on his behind.

So much history, so much knowledge.
Oh, man! I can never take it all in!

Each time I learn something new about my ancestors,
I feel as if I'm constantly being born...
Over and over again.

You see, the thing about it is,
If you keep your family's history alive,
Someone else might catch on fire
And be born
Three times, too!

REACHING AND GRABBING AT ME

Everybody reaching and grabbing,
      Reaching and grabbing at me.

I don't know what they see in me.
      I don't understand why so much jealousy.

That is something I never could be.
      To me it says insecurity.

Everybody reaching and grabbing at me.

Seek yourself.
      Be yourself.
           Reach and grab for yourself.

God made us all.
      Be the best you can be.

Be yourself.

Be yourself!

Reach and grab!
      Reach and grab!
           Be free of jealousy!

Then you will no longer be reaching
      And grabbing at me!

 AN AFRICAN ROCK

AN AFRICAN ROCK

If I could see though a Rock from South Africa,
What would I see?

Our ancestors extended their hand
To the white man
Many years ago
And the black man wound up in Slavery.

If I could see through a Rock from South Africa,
What would I see?

I would see Nelson Mandela
And other leaders fighting
To set South African people free.

If I could see through a Rock from South Africa,
What would I see?

Apartheid came to an end in 1994
And all races were able to vote
For the ANC.

They were free!

If I could see through a Rock from South Africa
What would I see?

A Black Man—Nelson Mandela—
Became president of his country.

DORIS DEAN HANNAH TURNER

If you could see through a Rock from South Africa,
What would you see?
Michael and Doris picked me up
So you can have a little piece of history.

So now, if someone says to you,
"It's just a Rock."
Tell them,
"This Rock has seen everything
In South Africa
That the rocks in America haven't seen."

 AN AFRICAN ROCK

MEMORIES THAT CANNOT BE ERASED

When we can no longer
See our loved one's face.

The memories that we
Shared cannot be erased.

The smile, the touch,
The warm embrace.

The hurt of disappointment.
The tears that dried upon your face.

The joy, the laughter.
Whatever you faced
Are memories that you cannot erase.

The bond, that we once shared,
May it be your family.
Perhaps a special friend,
A church member or two.

So choose your words and actions Carefully,
Because you are creating
Memories that cannot be erased.

DORIS DEAN HANNAH TURNER

TIME DOESN'T WAIT ON NO ONE

Time doesn't wait on no one.
Oh! You think it waits for you?
One day you were able to run and
Then time kept moving swiftly through.

Time doesn't wait on no one.
So you thought time wouldn't catch up with you?
Can you bend like you used to?
Can you jump up and down too?
Can you stay awake without taking a nap?
Oh! Time is catching up with you.

Is your hair getting gray? Is it falling out too?
Time doesn't wait on no one, not even you.

Our ancestors always said,
"Just keep on livin', Baby.
Time will catch up with you."

Does your neck look wrinkled?
Does your skin get dry too?

Can you hold you water
Or do you pee-pee in your pants too?

Does your sinus bother you
Since you reached 62?

AN AFRICAN ROCK

Did arthritis pay you a visit today?
Do you get constipated too?

Do your teeth crack when you're eating pecans?
Oh! You say, not you.

Just keep on livin', Baby.
Time doesn't wait on no one.

It will catch up with you.

A TASTE OF SOUTH AFRICA

Coffee, tea or cookies
Is what I brought back for you.

All the way from Cape Town, South Africa;
From across the deep blue sea.

People walking consistently to get to their destinations—
Work and school—no time for frolicking,
Because they have no time to play.

I took a trip to the market.
It was very busy, you see.

People selling their artwork,
Sculptures, jewelry and clothes.

The many talents that God has bestowed
Upon them.
He blesses their table every day.

So when you go to South Africa,
Make sure you support your brothers and sisters
As you go along the way.

Because they work hard to support their families
From day to day.

Don't forget the mommies on the street
Struggling to feed their children.

AN AFRICAN ROCK

Don't judge them,
Because you don't know their story.

It's only because of God's grace and glory
That you are not where they are today.

Just give from your heart.
It will come back to you someday.

DORIS DEAN HANNAH TURNER

A SOUTH AFRICAN TREE

A Tree with Character
And so much life.

Grouped in bunches,
Wild and free.

There's so much I can see
In a South African Tree.

Brown, beige, green & gold
Are the colors of the leaves
Of a South African Tree.

Some are young
And some are old.

Some are skinny. Some are fat.

Some are round and full
Of so much character
In that South African Tree.

They may not be different to you
But from my being,
I can see the character
In a South African Tree.

THE NATURE OF LIFE

A snake eagerly
Crosses the road.

A bird swoops and plucks
A fish from the sea.

Seaweed spreads
Across the wet sands of life.

The sea shells of different colors,
Shapes and sizes are beautifully
Made of different images.

The tiny ant that runs
Swiftly through the sand.

The plants so full of life
That surround us everywhere.

The waves that sweep
Us off our feet.

Thank you, Dear God, for
The nature of life
Presented in our presence.

THE OCEAN

As the big blue waves
Spread across the ocean,
The waves pushed everything
From the ocean.

Sea shells created
From oysters, clams, snails and mussels.

Seaweed is coughed
From the big blue ocean.

Some can be eaten
And some can be toxic.
So be careful of what comes from the ocean.

Copper, iron, salt, gravel and sand,
All which comes from the big blue ocean.

So, don't pollute the ocean with things that
Can be harmful.
Let's keep the big blue ocean free from debris.

 AN AFRICAN ROCK

NEVER TURN YOUR BACK ON THE OCEAN

Never turn your back on the ocean
    A big blue wave may be in action.

Never turn your back on the ocean.
    It just may catch you
    By surprise.

Never turn your back on the ocean.
    Grip yourself and
    Be as steady as you can.

Because no telling where you might land.

When you turn back around,
    the ocean becomes calm again.

SWISH, SWISH, SWISH

swish, swish, swish
tracks on the trail
from the shoes on the gravel

swish, swish, swish
tracks on the trail
some move slow and
some move fast

swish, swish, swish
walkers singing, praising and meditating
birds chirping
deer peeping through the trees
geese flying

swish, swish, swish
tracks on the trail

as i look towards the heavens
i can clearly see that
God is watching over me

 AN AFRICAN ROCK

LORD, I AM NOT PERFECT

Lord, I am not perfect.

Thank you for forgiveness.
Thank you for not putting our destiny in man's hands.

Lord, I am not perfect.

You look at our inner man and see goodness within.
Man looks at our sin and won't forgive.
Man doesn't have a heaven or a hell to put us in.

Lord, I am not perfect.

Thank you for forgiveness.

THE CHAINS OF LIFE

When the chains of life are shackling you,
You don't have a clue what it's like
To be free.

Bound up in the bowels of life.
Your thoughts of despair have got a grip on you.

Busy trying to take the shackles off that bind you
May take some time.

As you struggle through the process
To take off what binds you.

Figure out what it is that's holding you.
Grip it; cast it out into the sea of despair.
Yes, those shackles of life that bound you.

Then you can be free from the chains of life
That used to shackle you.

 AN AFRICAN ROCK

RESILIENT

To be resilient is a gift
That most people do not possess,
Or yet even understand.

Most can't find their own
Happiness from within.

Tests and trials in life may come and go,
But it's how you stand the tests of life that
Makes you glow.

To be resilient is not a curse.
We must fight the principalities of darkness.

So, be resilient...it's a gift.

Don't allow people to make you feel it's a curse.

Just keep on living life and thank God for the gift.

THANKSGIVING

A holiday no one should spend alone…

People preparing turkey, chicken, duck, hens and ham.
Macaroni & cheese, collard greens, potato salad,
Dressing and cranberry sauce too.

Plenty of cakes and pies made from Granny's
Special recipe from generations ago.

Make sure you invite family and friends,
Especially those who live alone.

Don't forget to fill your home with Love,
Just the way Mama used to do.
No one was left out. She spread her Love
Through and through.

Otherwise, you will lose what Mama taught you
In what's most important about Thanksgiving.

People were all over the house
Just to eat that special meal that is only cooked
once a year.

Fun and games were always played,
With plenty of laughing and sharing with
Family and friends.

 AN AFRICAN ROCK

Don't forget to spread your Love.
Thanksgiving is not about you.

It's about caring and sharing your Love
The way you prepare your food.

Good hospitality is very important to keep the
Generations together,
Spreading Love
To everyone's lives you touch throughout the
Year too.

DORIS DEAN HANNAH TURNER

COURAGE TO BE FREE

Shaving the hair off my head is one of the most
Courageous but yet, the most difficult decision
I ever had to make.

When my eyebrows got thin,
I just took a pencil and drew them in.

When my underarm hair was too long,
I just took a razor and shaved it off.

Thinning of my Cuda Kat. What did I do?
No problem I just took that off, too.

Now I'm down to the hair on my legs. What do I do?
Take that razor and shave that hair off,
Wouldn't you?

Before I took my hair off, I looked like Bozo the Clown.
So, I decided to take the final step. I know I'm
Brave enough too.

Don't cry, don't get depressed.
Just do what you have to do.

After 20 years of watching my hair thin;
Wearing hats, scarves, and head pieces too.

I'm so tired of covering my head,

 AN AFRICAN ROCK

I don't know what to do!

I'm going to keep my head up and a big smile
On my face because I know hair doesn't define
Me nor you.

Don't be judgmental. One day it could happen to you!
Not looking for approval. I just want you to know.

I'm a Bold, Bald, Beautiful, Black Woman
And today, I see me.

I'm not hiding anymore.
I have Courage.

I. AM. FREE!

A ROSE

A rose is one of the most beautiful flowers
That God has created.

We consider you as one of God's most beautiful
Women who exemplifies a Christian's life.

You are a rose with many petals
Which represent the many talents
That God has given you.

You are the soil that holds the plant together
Here at Joseph Campau.

You are the rain that falls upon the rose petals
Which brings life
To all whose lives you touch.

Your smile, your love and concern for others
Is like the sunshine that provides the sparkle
That defines the beauty of a rose.

 AN AFRICAN ROCK

OUR PASTOR IS HUMAN

Our Pastor is human.
He laughs, talks, sings and has emotions too.

Our pastor is human.
He sometimes feels discouraged and all alone.

Our pastor is human.
Oh yes! He has needs that money can buy.

Our Pastor Is human.
He is sometimes tempted, and has trials and
Tribulations too.

Listen, Pastor! When you feel discouraged,
Jesus will never leave you.

You have needs that money can buy.
God will supply all your needs.

You are sometimes tempted and you have
Trials and tribulations.
Just stand, and the crown of life will be waiting
For you.

WHO

Who are you?

Do you know who you are?
Do you know whose you are?

Who **are** you?

Do you know what you're doing?
Do you realize what you're saying?
Do you know where you're going?
Do you know where you came from?
Do you know when you are going to finish?
Do you know why you did that?
Do you know how you are going to get there?
Do you know who you look like?
Do you know who you act like?

Who are **you**?

ABOUT THE AUTHOR

Doris Dean Hannah Turner is a gifted and multi-talented entrepreneur. Her credits include, "Dolls Exquisitely Dressed by Doris" which were featured and showcased in numerous Detroit Public Schools. She is one of the co-founders of "Lady Butterflies," a young ladies' mentorship program at Chandler Park Academy. She is a native of Mt. Clemens, Michigan.

Her parents were the late Alexander and Annie Bell Hannah. They birthed and inspired her to become this phenomenal and sophisticated lady. She had the impartation of entrepreneurship from her father, who was a business owner in the community, and great foundational principals for parenting from her mother.

She surrendered her life to Christ when she was 18 years old. She is especially grateful to the Greater Morning Star Missionary Baptist Church for their bible study group. It really impacted her Christian experience with Jesus Christ. She is eternally indebted to Mother Bernice Whiteside for her spiritual growth and development. Her role in her life was paramount and life-changing.

Doris' life was transformed at 19 years of age when she met and fell in love with Michael Turner, Sr. They married shortly after this love connection. God granted and blessed them with three dynamic children, five grandchildren and one great-grandchild.

She was overjoyed immensely with 44 years of partnership, love and devotion from her husband Michael until his passing in 2019.

God has breathed life into her ideals and given her courage to follow through as an entrepreneur. Her comedic personality, Lady Dean, talks about the things we don't often want to discuss or face.

Her church affiliation and membership is with Joseph Campau Avenue, Church of God located on the Northeast side of Detroit.

Doris' interests includes traveling, shopping, bike riding, cooking and meeting family. Additionally, she likes planning family reunions, special events and making people laugh!

She pursued and earned a Certificate in Ministry from the California School of Ministry at the age of 40. She later earned her certification in the rules of etiquette behavior from "The Etiquette Institute" in St. Louis, MO.

LET'S KEEP IN TOUCH!

@DORIS.HANNAHTURNER

@DORISTURNER

@DORISHANNAHTURNER

TURNERDD62@GMAIL.COM

Doris Dean Hannah Turner is available for speaking engagements. Please contact her via e-mail or through her social media channels.

www.ingramcontent.com/pod-product-compliance
Lightning Source LLC
Chambersburg PA
CBHW042120100526
44587CB00025B/4133